The Science Fair

by Kama Einhorn
illustrated by David Bergstein

Editorial Offices: Glenview, Illinois • Parsippany, New Jersey • New York, New York
Sales Offices: Needham, Massachusetts • Duluth, Georgia • Glenview, Illinois
Coppell, Texas • Ontario, California • Mesa, Arizona

Every effort has been made to secure permission and provide appropriate credit for photographic material. The publisher deeply regrets any omission and pledges to correct errors called to its attention in subsequent editions.

Unless otherwise acknowledged, all photographs are the property of Scott Foresman, a division of Pearson Education.

Photo locators denoted as follows: Top (T), Center (C), Bottom (B), Left (L), Right (R), Background (Bkgd)

8(B) ©Roger Ressmeyer/Corbis

ISBN: 0-328-13262-4

6 7 8 9 10 V010 14 13 12 11 10 09 08 07

"We're having a science fair," Miss Heath said. "Each grade will enter a project. We'll work together. People from the village will come to watch us at the fair."

"What can we do?" Miss Heath asked.

"Let's make a new kind of shoe!" said Joe.

"Let's study apes!" cried Lana.

"We're studying volcanoes," said Billy.
"Let's build a volcano model."

"Yes! We can show how a volcano
erupts," the others agreed.

We got an empty soda bottle. We
molded dough around it. We tried to
make it pretty. We filled the bottle with
warm water and red food coloring. We
added soap and baking soda.

At the fair, we added vinegar to our volcano. It erupted perfectly. The red foam looked like hot lava flowing down the sides.

Guess who won first place? We did!

Everyday Experiments

Scientists around the world study and work together on different kinds of experiments. Studying volcanoes helps us understand how they form and erupt. It can also help us identify the warning signs of an eruption. Knowing the warning signs can help us save the lives of people who live near volcanoes. All scientists experiment, test their ideas, and draw conclusions from their studies.

Scientists study maps to help people before a volcano erupts.